TIDES OF INFLUENCE

Best Wishes
Stella Humphreys

by
Stella Humphreys

Published by BWW Publishing

First BWW Printing, September 1996
Printed by Ted Weiss Printing, Langhorne, PA

Illustrations by Olga Perlman

Photographs by Dayna Otto

ISBN

0-9654037-0-X

Printed in the United States of America

Acknowledgment

Sixteen years ago, while I was still living in Westchester, my next door neighbor and dear friend Betsy Whitmore drove me to the hospital when my third child was about to be born. She stayed with me until my husband arrived.

At that time, I had not even written one poem. I was too busy living my poetry. Well now Betsy is again, the driving force. She has removed all the stumbling blocks and she is the financial vehicle for me to deliver my dream to publish my poems.

I love to express myself with words but there are no words that will adequately express my gratitude to Betsy. I will just say I am incredibly fortunate to have a friend who has been consistently enthusiastic, supportive and generous.

Forward

The majority of my poems are written in the first person. Many of them are my personal experiences and philosophical beliefs. Others are feelings or experiences that friends have shared with me. The expression and intensity of their feelings impacted me, so much so, that I felt I could write about their experiences in the first person. I thank each of them for their openness and honesty. I hope I have done justice to their feelings.

My poems are verbal photographs. They comfort me and give vivid clarity to my deepest feelings. I hope as you read my words you will reflect on your own life and appreciate the uniqueness and importance of your experiences. Let them be the catalyst for change and growth.

I wish each of you personal fulfillment.

TO YOU
WHO SHARED YOURSELF WITH ME
OF US

THESE POEMS ARE BORN

S.

THE TIDES OF INLUENCE

I am driftwood,
Floating on ocean,
Carried by tides.

I accept it all,
calms and squalls.

I have become what I need to be
To exist in my world.

I do more than accept, endure and survive,
I change and grow with

THE TIDES OF INFLUENCE. . .

TABLE OF CONTENTS

THE CHANGING TIDE

BY DEFINITION

I will not be defined by others.
    Only I can define myself.

I will not make anyone else's choices.
Their choices will not fit my heart.

My heart's instincts never fail me.
    I do not fear rejection
        Because

The gifts I give are not trinkets of barter.
    My gifts are gifts of love,
        Given on open hands,
        Extended from open arms.

With each offering, what I have to give
    Grows magically.

I am healthier, stronger,
    and SO much richer . . .

REBIRTH

I have chosen the path;
    it is narrow.

I have followed the rules;
    they bind.

I have never questioned;
    now I have no answers.

I have followed the leaders;
    I am lost

I have done the right thing;
    I am empty.

Now, I dare to be different;
    I am frightened.

But I take the next step;
    I grow stronger.

I begin to feel a new power;
    I emerge to appreciate life.

ONCE UPON A TIME

Red Riding Hood,
Frightened of all the wolves and obstacles.

Cinderella,
Self-proclaimed plain and dull.

Sleeping Beauty,
Awakened after forty years.

No princely kiss,
Slapped by reality.

IN THE MIRROR

Who is that woman?
Where did the girl go?
    Who married life with a passion,
    Who was pregnant with ideals,
    Who labored with the inconsistencies,
    Who gave birth to reality?

Who is that woman?
Where did the girl go?
    Who had the round cheeks,
    the unfurrowed brow, the wide-eye
    innocence?

Where did the girl go?
Who is that woman?
    With the lines of laughter, the
    furrows of worry?

Where did the girl go?
She IS that woman,
    In a gown of experience, veiled in the
    passage of time.

THE CHILD IN ME

The child in me
Beneath adult facade
Waiting for its cue

Wisdom in the child
Finding humor wherever

Call me a fool
Wise fool

Nurture this child
Who seaons my life

    With humor and perceptive

KALEIDOSCOPE

Relationships,
Creating patterns, swirls,
Bright and dark.

People intersect,
Change with innuendo.

Feelings whirl purple.
Yellow, loving circles, disappear
Becoming cool blue square obligations.

Look again,
Passion red outlines
This kaleidoscope world.
Emotions, color and shape, ever-changing
Purpose and beauty is the difference

NEVER SO MUCH AS NOW

All at once
I am soft as steel,
       strong as sand;
          A woman.

Be there for me,
I will not lean,

    Hold me
But no too tightly,
I need to breath.

    Talk;
I will listen.

    Lecture;
I will dream of someone else,
       somewhere else,

Who will listen
        But
Not lecture.

All at once,
I need to be needed
        And
Not to be needed.

Never so much as now,
I need to be . . .

JOURNEY

Where I am on my journey,
No longer a cinder block in a cinder block
wall.

I am

A jagged stone on a foreign beach.

EXPLORER

Born at last!

BEACH GLASS

Life tosses us upon the shore,
     Again and again.
Starting out rough-edged shards,
     Untempered splinters,
Shattering at the feet of experience.

Life tosses us upon the shore,
     Again and again.
Sands of conflict wear away
our - at first - unyielding sharp edges,
Tumbled about in the turbulence
     Of each new day.

Life tosses us upon the shore,
     Again and again.
We become treasures, beautiful smooth
jewels,
     Brilliant pieces of multicolor
     Beach Glass,

Creations of the inevitable power,

     THE TIDAL EXPERIENCE OF LIFE.

FIRE

That fire
> of almost fifty years,
> empowers me to meet the storms.

That fire
> that never dims
> and never allows darkness in my heart.

That fire
> that melts away icy disappointment
> and lights my way.

That fire
> that welcomes everyone
> and sends visitors away with lit candles.

That fire
> that will never die.

That fire
> I am.

That fire
> is me.

LOST AT SEA

WHERE THE TIME GOES

And this is the way the time goes.
I long to grow.
I wish the days to go.
    And they do.
And the holidays, and the seasons,
And I wish it was Spring,
    No, Summer
    No, Fall
And no, I wish it was Christmas.
And this is the way the time goes.
And I wish I was 18,
    No, 21.
No, on my own, with a place of my own.
And now, I wish the children were grown.
And I wish I was free.
And this is the way the time goes.
And now I am old and alone.
And where does the time go?

WASHED IN LIGHT

Each evening,
Driving along at dusk,
    Along familiar streets
Streaks of clouds at sunset
Each lighted window

        Renews,
            The pain,
                The loss,

Driven to this pilgrimage
Always on the outside looking in.

        Remembering.

Selfishly, holding on to the pain.
All that's left is the pain.

Death has stolen

            My Mother
            My Sister

Each evening,
Driving along at dusk,

Along familiar streets

Streaks of clouds at sunset
I build a room of memories, in my soul

For you, My Mother

For you, My Sister

What we had

Will always be

Safe,

Remembered,

Washed in light.

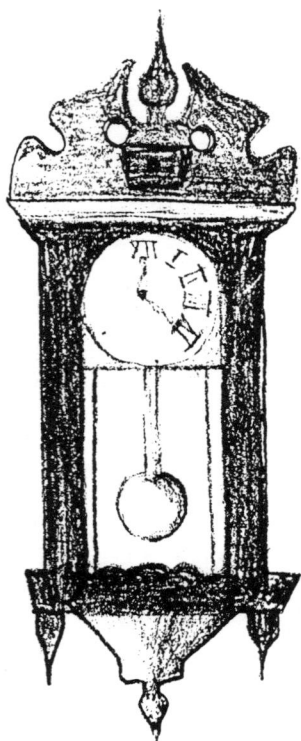

DAD

Dad won't be coming home.
    5:30 on the stoop
    I wait for Dad.
    Cooking scents and sounds,
    Caruso reaches me from Grandpa's
    record player.

Dad won't be coming home.
    I am young but understand:
    Dad's pale face,
    Mom's strained voice,
    Haulted conversations,
    Whispered word –
            cancer . . .

Dad won't be coming home.
    5:30 on the stoop
    Dad's time
    Erase it from the clock.

FOR IRENE AND HER FRIEND

A.I.D.S.,
    The leper's bell on leaden chain,
    Strangling your victims.
No sooner named,
    You hurl them down.
    Crushing hopes, dreams, future.
Discrimination and isolation, the cruelest
symptoms.
Does the dying begin within or
Are we all a part of the affliction?

If anger's heat could destroy,
I would free your sickened slaves.
    Send you back to hell.
And with that strength,
    Blow healthy breath of life into
    Fragile lungs and failing cells.
Let love renew,
    Waxen skin to healthy glow.
Give back the hope,
    The Dreams,
        The Future.

MY FAVORITE
SHELLS

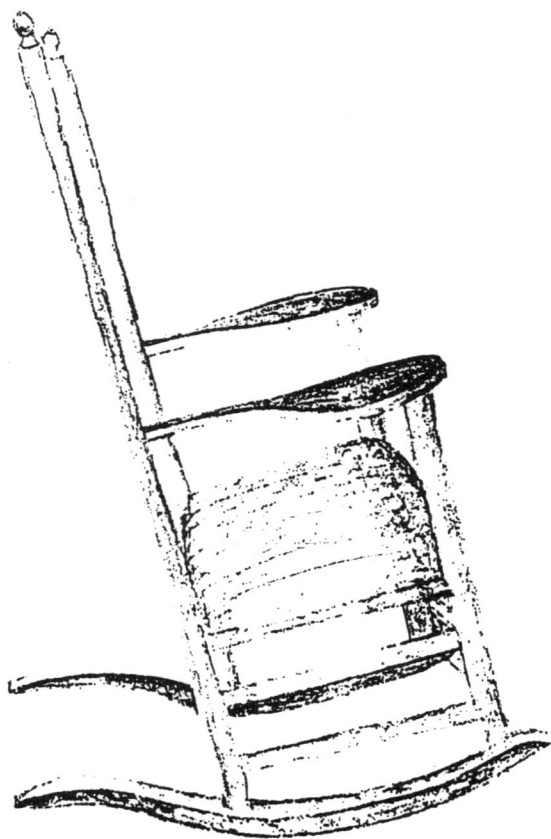

NINE WONDROUS MONTHS

Pregnant, the doctor said.
Pregnant with emotion,
Wonder and Joy.

At first,
Scientific knowledge, my only proof,
Then, mornings verify my state.

Impatiently, I wait for you to touch me.
First flutter from within, so brief,
Was it real or my imagining?

I greet you each morning, "I Love You".
I rock you each afternoon,
Dreaming of our first meeting.

As you grow, I am so proud of my misshapen body,
Perfect for your needs.

I read all the recommended books.
Your progress fills my waking thoughts.

Doctor lets me hear your heart;
My own heart skips a beat.

At home again, in our rocker,
I speak softly, tracing small circles on my belly.
You acknowledge me.
Your motion slow, a stretch, perhaps.

Contentment
We sit and rock, dreaming of the future.

FATE

Born to me at three months old.
How can it be?
"A baby boy", they said,
"He needs love and a home".
I have love and a home.
So he came to be conceived.
Delivered to his father's arms.
Another miracle,
Grown now. Everyone says, "Why, he looks
just like his Dad!"
Fate.

RIGHT-BRAINED CHILD

Precious child
Wordless child

Tender, touching, loving child

Out of balance
Out of step
Out of sync

But never without my love

Labeled child
Emotional child
Right-brained child

Living in a left-brained world

What will become of you?

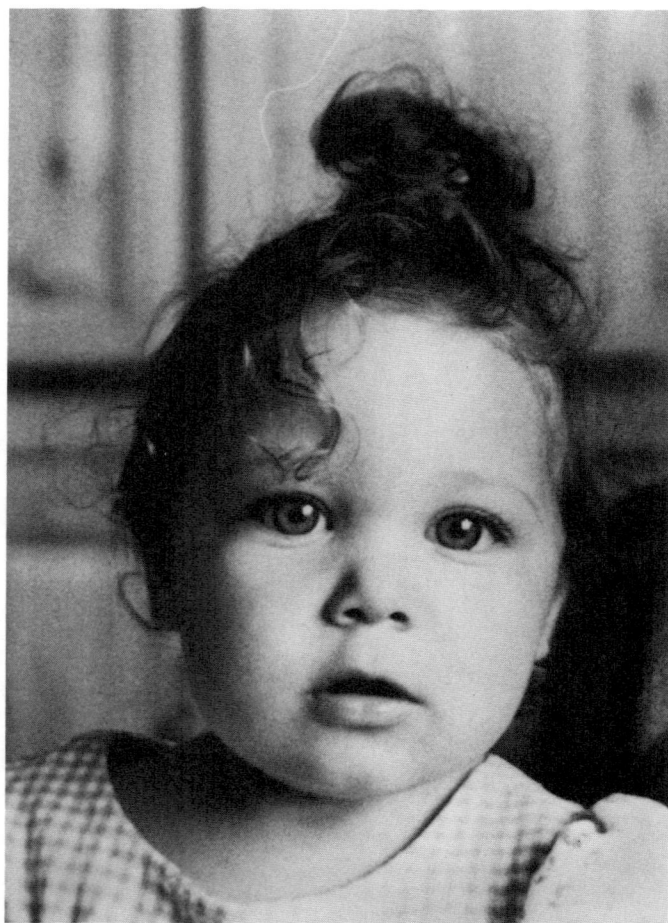

CHILD OF MY CHILD

Tiny things, soft pastels,
     Soon
I will be buying
     For
The child of my child.

Remembered joy at his birth.
My anticipation magnified –
     Another generation.

Sweet smell of innocence,
     Tiny hand soon to be
Curled around my finger.

A tender closeness,
My son and his wife,
     Brings me joy.

Three generations wait
For this new life,
     This child,
Already swaddled in unconditional love.

REALIGNING

This is for you my son.

At the beginning, you fit perfectly within my body.
But now, at sixteen, you don't fit within my mind.
We don't have to be mirror images.

Just fluid friends.

I admire your intelligence.

I am startled by your intuition.
      Complex Child,

I love you but don't always like you.
I think you feel the same way about me.

       I'm not sure.

I've never really known you

But want to.

Take your special place within my heart.

DRIFTWOOD

LONG BEACH ISLAND

Long Beach Island, barrier reef island,
Protects mainland from Atlantic,
Protects me from mainland.

I cross the causeway, shedding schedules
and worries.
My only appointments
    Sunrise on the beach,
      Sunset on the bay,
        finding the perfect shell.

Long Beach Island, barrier reef island,
Cloak of serenity, sounds and light unique
each season . . .

Long Beach Island, barrier reef island,
Protects mainland from Atlantic,
Protects me from mainland.

BEAUTIFUL TYRANT

Perfect features,
        imperfect soul

Beautiful eyes,
        see only self

Full lovely lips,
        utter vicious hurtful words

Sought after but,
        self-absorbed

Pampered,
        Envied,

                Wanted,

                        Empty

PRECIPICE

On this precipice
I am clear and strong.
My doubts left far below.
My thoughts refined to vision,
Knowing all I need to know.

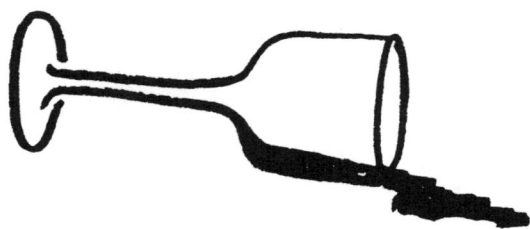

YOU SHARE THE CUP

Broken promises,
There is no answer.

I cannot attain a state of numbness.

I am tricked by my solution into vivid
images.

Your face as potent as the wine I've
taken.

I feel the pain.

    I drink the wine.

        You share the cup . . .

IMAGINATION

Carefree, wingless flight
Above the roof tops
Things dreams are made of.

Floating, silent flight
Freedom in the clouds,
Free-falling,
Landing as light as a feather,
Stepping out of imagination . . .

THE MAZE

My anger creates walls;
       I am imprisoned.

My anger clouds my mind;
       I am a maze of indecision.

My anger will ignite and destroy,
      The fragile parchment of my soul.

TWENTY YEARS ON THE JOB

His job made him feel;

> Worn as a piece of driftwood,

> Empty as the beach in January,

> Predictable as the tides.

IN THE HEARTLAND

Fragmented lives
Shattered emotions

Unearthed anger
Smoldering revenge

Rescue the stability
Rescue the security

Bury the terror
Mourn the children

Young and old

EXPLORER

Explorer
Traveling the galaxy
No fuel spent
My telescope enables
Unencumbered endless flight.

Telescope
Vessel to new worlds
Planets
  Stars
    Moons
      Sun
Cradled by Little Dipper
Brave against Great Bear

I greet Orion

Waxing and waning
The moon a soothing respite
Like Columbus in search of the new world
Adventurer challenged by possibilities
A new horizon

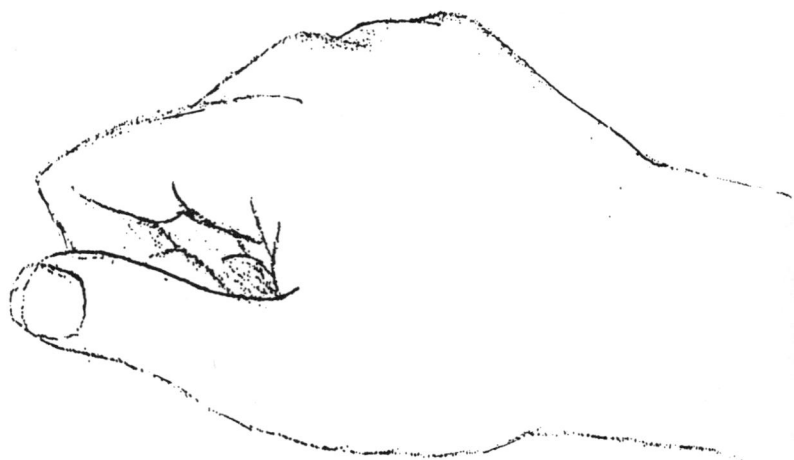

HEALING HANDS

See
>the texture of the skin,
>The width and length,
>Each line and vein.

Healing hands

Powerful hands,
Warm hands,
Tenderness and compassion
Flow through those hands.

Healing hands

Palms up, open hands,
Welcoming,
>Nurturing,
>>Giving hands.

Healing hands

SEASONS OF GREEN

In fall the green is faded and fallen.
All but the green squash, peppers and beans we
harvest and enjoy.

But winter brings different greens.
Christmas firs to go with Christmas wishes.
Greenbacks disappear in all directions.
Green velvet dresses bring in the new year.

And then, the waiting, the anticipation, the need
for spring. The pale of new leaves, new grass as
the earth warms. Green frogs sing their love
songs through the night. Houses surrounded like
paintings by their new green frames.

Then quickly, summer brings a new face.
Hills wear their dark green masks.
The sweet watermelon scent of freshly cut grass

Moss thickens on the trees.
Everything is hushed by the lush greenery.

Until
In the fall the green fades and falls.

TANGO

Second chance
Chance
To take

Take
The flight

Flight
To dance

Dance
The tango

Tango
On
The
Tail
Of
The
World

Come dance with me.

LASTING BEAUTY

Beauty at a distance
Seen with judgmental eyes, critical eyes,
Will fade and decay.

Come closer
A whisper's distance
Where expressed thoughts create
Lasting beauty, eternal beauty
In the wealth of words spoken.

A figure of curves,
Breasts, slow rise and fall
A mesmerizing pulchritude,
Created by faith in humanity.

Permanent perfection
Cast in strength,
Preserved in integrity.
A beauty made immortal
By its sensuous honesty.

AGAINST THE TIDES

LOVE WITH CAUTION

Love with caution –
    An inconsistent premise.

Love cannot live in caution.

Love cannot be conceived in caution
    Caution can neither feel nor love.
    Caution is a coward.

It has no pulse, no faith, no trust.

Caution has no place in the heart's mind.

    Love with Valor,

For honest emotion has only one enemy,

    Caution Born of Expectations.

SILENCE

Immersed in tears, behind a smiling mask.
    My thoughts sanctioned;
    My words censored;
    My heart mourning;

No place for me to grieve.
I place my love upon the grave, without regrets.
How long before it withers.
No one to nourish the fragile petals of my
emotions.
      I struggle to survive
        Against
The choking vines of small minds
          And
        Worst of all,
        the silence

Like a fertile field gone barren.

TO ALL THE JUDYS

Our mothers' promised in their fairy tales
    A happy ending.

So, we gave birth to our babies;
      We cherished these children.
Who sealed the bond to the men we lie
with.

      Committing to the dream

        Then

Our marriages gave birth to lies and
deceptions.

No rhythm to the labor.

Just tortured waves of disillusionment
infecting us.

We bear it all.

Hoping to turn the tide of broken promises,
Only to have our trust and faith
Ripped from our wombs.

Leaving us bleeding dreams.
Leaving us to mourn our aborted trust.
Leaving us so damaged

All we can bear are faint memories
Of our mothers' promised happy-ever-
afters.

A small seed within us, still pregnant with
hope.

A cursed blessing a woman's strength.

WALLS

Our eyes connect
Touch without touching
Have not had
Cannot have
    Separated by
        High walls
        Thick walls
        Entombing walls
Built of moral fiber
Learned in childhood
Knowing you
I have flourished
Without you I am
    Isolated
        Empty
Without your voice
Flesh shrinks away from bone

Your thoughts nourish
Like water I gulp
Excess pouring down
    My face
        My throat
            My breasts
Covering my body

Moral walls imprison
I exist machine-like
My body functions
My mind withers
Separated by   WALLS

Bound together   A P A R T.

VACANT HEART

New territory
This vacant heart

Vanished voice
Valid promises erased
Replaced by
Unclear images of unkind shadows

This vacant heart
Swept clean of dreams

Echoes empty misty memories.

SECRETS MERMAIDS HAVE SHARED

TABERNACLE OF DREAMS

I am intuition, instinct and emotion.

I am guardian of your hopes.

I am cradle of your fantasies.

I am tabernacle of your dreams.

I revel in your humanity.

OUT OF THE ASHES

You came upon the thick gray ash;
    You noticed there -
       An ember.

Others had walked this way,
But none had seen the glow beneath the
gray.
           You stayed,

Placing branches of tender words
    Upon the glow.

You fanned the flame
     With
Breaths of encouragement,

    You were a shelter

From the harsh rains of others'
expectations,

From the icy winds of disapproval;
They would surely extinguish the light.

Now,

You will be warmed by the fire;

You will never be alone in the dark;

You will look into the heart

Of these dancing flames;

There you will see,

Your eternal torch ... called me.

OASIS

I am an oasis.

Drink from this pool,

Or reflect in it.

All that I am is yours,

An Oasis for your body and soul.

FAITH

Technicolor dreams

Stopped by black and white neurosis

Whispered shyness

Silent screaming

> Wordless pages

> Finally written

By uncommon belief in me

By an uncommon you

OF NOTHING REAL

An overwhelming loss
     of nothing real
but my real feelings.

Under the microscope
     a middle-aged little girl
with dreams un-dreamt
promises, never made, to be kept.

An overwhelming loss
     of nothing real
but my real feelings.

Under the microscope
     an open wound
created by me now endured by me.

An overwhelming loss
     of nothing real
but my real feelings.

I sit with a casket of love no place to mourn
the loss.

What loss?

Of nothing real

buy my real feelings.

A nameless pain, I have no right to feel

but deserve to endure.

A little girl in a middle-aged mask
under the microscope

with my real feelings.

SYMPHONY OF TWO SPIRITS

A distant chord

The word dance draws them together

Rhythm of thought

Punctuated by laughter

Creates a melody

    As synchronized as their heartbeats

A symphony born

    Harmony of two spirits

Played infinitely in their soul

Forever friends.

CELEBRATION

My affection does not qualify or separate,

Your strengths from your fears.

I appreciate the sum of all your traits.

Vulnerability makes you lovable.

Sensitivity makes you admirable.

There is nothing I would change;

Knowing you is a celebration.

ADVICE

Advice, unlike experience, whispers.

Experience echoes.

Advice paints in water colors.

Experience brands.

Advice is bleached in the sun.

Experience is etched in stone.

Advice is tucked in a drawer.

Experience is worn like armor.

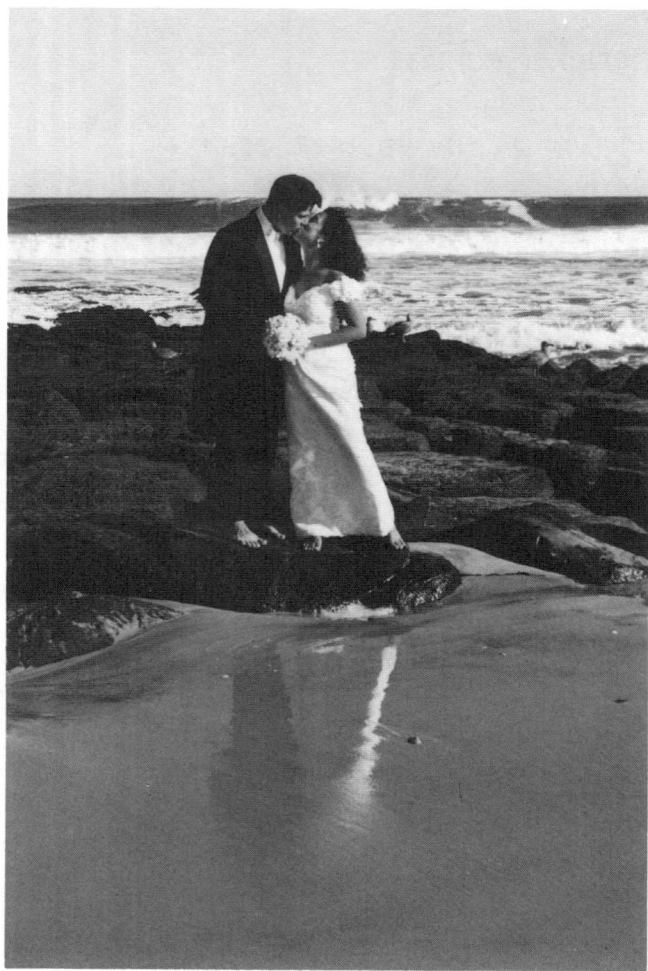

A SEA OF LOVE

A gift
Generous and powerful as the sea

Ever-changing
Blue-Green-Joy
Misty-Calm
White-Capped-Passion
Gray-Days-Of-Disagreement
A necessary balance

A lighthouse of promises to return to
Worthy of constant vigilance
Accept the squalls
Ride the waves of passion

A sea of love
Let it caress and console you
As its warm waves wash over you
Embrace the tides of commitment and trust
Have faith in its majesty

A Sea Of Love
Bountiful

TRUST

Controlled too often, love will escape.

Held too tightly, love is crushed.

Watched too closely, love will vanish.

Given time and space, love will grow.

Given freedom, love will reach new heights.

Given respect, love will be strengthened.

Love through trust

Trust in Love

LIFE

Life is a demanding, insatiable lover,

I will give him my best.

The future is a question I will answer

And a challenge I will meet.

Nothing less will do.

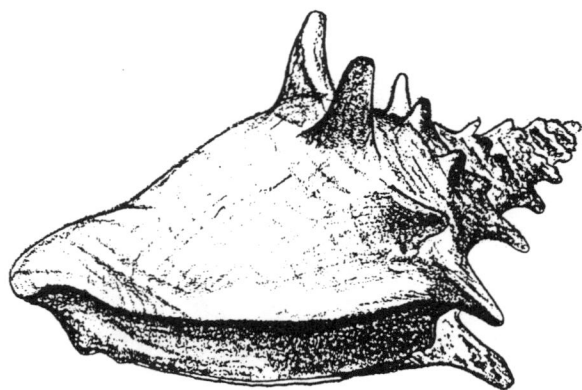

RHYTHM

From the first heartbeat of the unborn child,
A rhythm.
And the mother rocks a rhythm,
In the sing-song of a lullaby,
A necessary rhythm.
And in the music is a rhythm.
It pulls me to my feet..
My body feels the rhythm.
All at once I feel complete.
And on any day
I'm comforted by the rhythm of the sea,
As I lie upon the shore.
And as I stroke the warm dark skin
An innocent comfort is created
By the rhythm of my touch.

And since time began
An ever-present rhythm,
As two bodies in the darkness
Become an ecstasy complete.
And so, we come full circle to
The first heartbeat of the unborn child,
A rhythm.

About The Author

Stella Humphreys was born in Bronx, New York. She moved with her family to Ocean County, New Jersey, when she was 13. Here began Stella's deep connection to the ocean.

After marrying young and having her family, at 40 she returned to college where she majored in English with a concentration in writing. It was there she was fortunate to find supportive teachers who recognized her abilities and urged her to pursue her writing.

Today she draws inspiration from and divides her time among family homes in Hopewell Junction, New York; Long Beach Island, New Jersey and Calabash, North Carolina. She has been married for 27 years, has four sons and one granddaughter.

Ms. Humphreys is currently at work on her first novel.